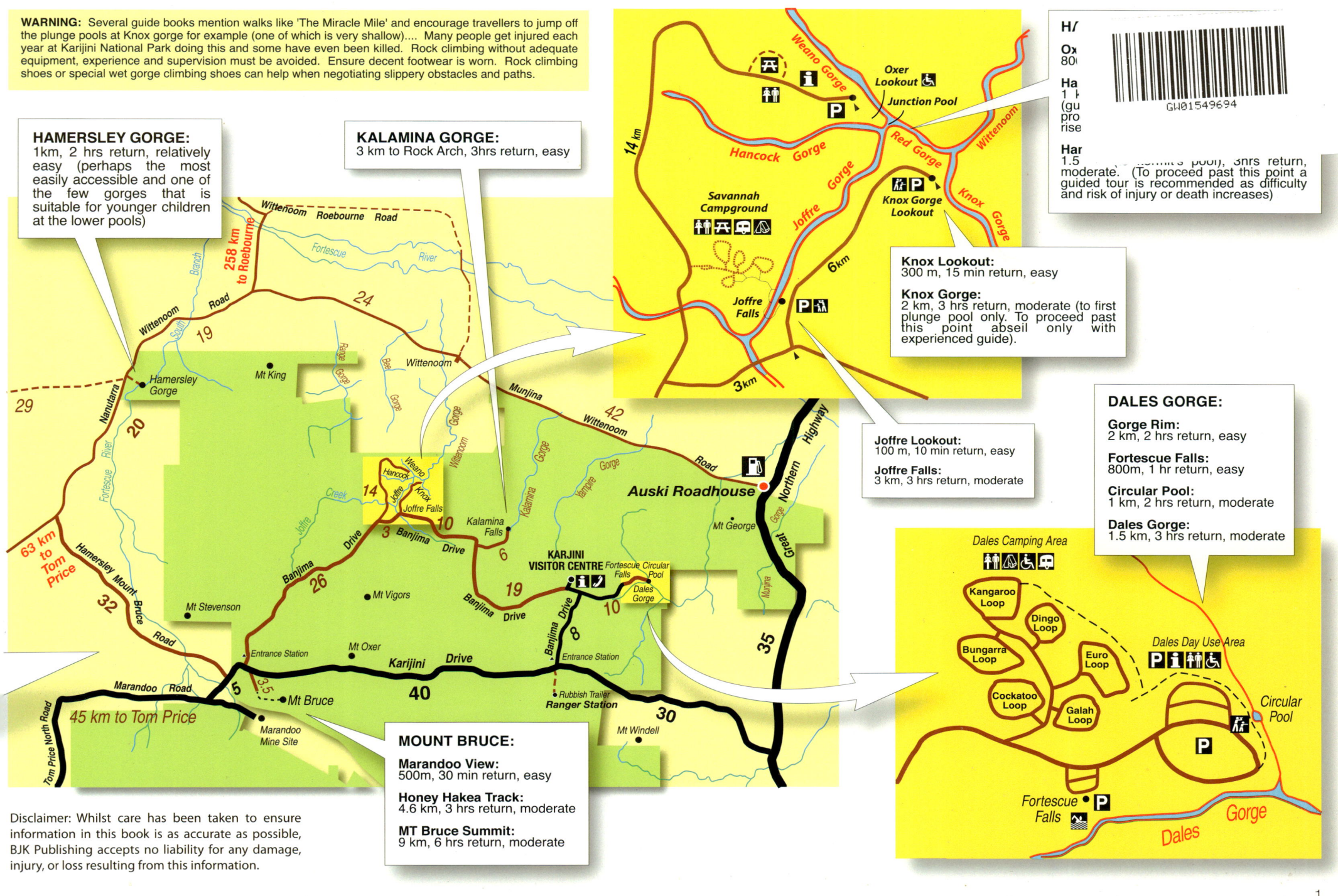

THE PILBARA

Western Australia's Pilbara region spans approximately 500,000 square kilometers of the north-western corner of Australia. Known for its rugged scenery and rock formations dated half as old as the earth, over two billion years old.

There is much to see in the Pilbara. From 80 Mile Beach, to the palm lined oasis of Millstream (featured toward the end of this book), to the legendary Whim Creek Pub. There is the historic coastal town of Cossack, Australia's hottest town of Marble Bar, the blow holes of Point Quobba, the Dampier Archipelago of 42 islands, and the Rudall River National Park on the edge of the Great Sandy Desert - arguably the most remote national park in Australia, and much more.

KARIJINI NATIONAL PARK

This pictorial souvenir book mainly focuses on one of the Pilbara's most popular attractions which is Karijini National Park set in the heart of the Pilbara in the Hamersley Range. The Banyjima, Yinhawangka and Kurrama Aboriginal people, the traditional owners, originally gave the Hamersley Range the name 'Karijini'. In the accessible northern half of the park, the deep shady chasms with cool clear flowing water and rocks with an intense range of fold lines, patterns & colours leave tourists describing it like no place on earth.

Each gorge is very different, some with narrow spiraling speed slide like water ways and plunge pools several meters high. It is no doubt one of the best 'must see' national parks in Australia.

Perhaps Karijini is not for everyone as there can be a lot of climbing and walking involved, often over slippery rocks. Each gorge has varying grades of difficulty so some will be more suitable than others. Guided tours are recommended. For those who are able to do the gorge walks, Karijini will be a breathtaking experience.

Hamersley Gorge

Hamersley Gorge

Hamersley Gorge

Spa Pool, Hamersley Gorge

12 Circular Pool, Dales Gorge

Circular Pool, Dales Gorge

Circular Pool, Dales Gorge

18 Fortescue Falls, Dales Gorge

Fortescue Falls, Dales Gorge

Fern Pool

Kermit's Pool, Hancock Gorge

Regan's Pool, Hancock Gorge

Kermit's Pool, Hancock Gorge

'The Chute' Hancock Gorge

Hancock Gorge

Weano Gorge

Handrail Pool, Weano Gorge

KNOX GORGE - has claimed many serious injuries over the years. A guided tour is strongly recommended as it is the only way to see the awesome end pools properly & safely.

After an initial steep decent & an hour+ walk the gorge narrows to a spiralling 'speed slide' with a drop off several metres high that you can't climb back up without abseiling equipment. This is where you need to turn back.

HAMERSLEY RANGE –
FIne grained iron and silica rich sediment accumulated on an ancient sea floor 2,500 million years ago. Over many millions of years, these iron rich deposits were transformed by pressure from further sediment into hard bedded rock. A rapid drop in sea level caused rivers of erosion that helped create the Pilbara landscape and gorges of Karijini we see today.

Iron Ore was discovered in the Pilbara region in the 1800's but exploitation of the resource was not feasible at the time due to the isolation and ruggedness of the area. In the 1950's pastoralist, Langley Hancock believed it was possible and recommended his ideas to Rio Tinto. His efforts soon instigated the discovery of one of the richest iron ore bodies in the world. The Hamersley Iron mine at Mount Tom Price was commissioned in 1962 with several other massive mines now running exporting over 68 million tonnes each year transforming the economy of Western Australia.

MILLSTREAM CHICHESTER NATIONAL PARK – spans 200,000 hectares.

The mostly arid landscape of sharply rising escapements, spinifex hills, and tree-lined watercourses contrasts greatly to the lush oasis of the Millstream wetlands. The area has a cultural importance to the Yinjibarndi people who lived in the area long before white man came.

The pastoral lease for Millstream was first taken up in 1865 and was an active pastoral station for more than 100 years. It changed hands several times and in it's prime ran 55,000 sheep over 400,000 hectares. The current homestead was built in 1920.

The homestead is now a visitor centre which is operated by the Department of Environment & Conservation (D.E.C.). There are now displays in many rooms dedicated to the Yinjibarndi people, the early settlers and the surrounding environment. Well worth a look. The cliff lookout shown on the following spread was taken early in the morning which is arguably the best time. It looks totally different at midday & perhaps a lot less spectacular.

Beyond Karijini - Cliff Lookout, Millstream N.P.

Beyond Karijini - Mt Nameless, Tom Price

Page 4 - 5 KR02	Page 6 - 7 KR07	Page 8 KR05	Page 9 KR03	Page 38 KR20	Page 16 KR32
Hamersley Gorge Pool	Hamersley Gorge	Hamersley Gorge	Hamersley Gorge	Oxer Lookout	Circular Pool
Page 10 - 11 KR13	Page 12 - 13 KR25	Page 14 - 15 KR14	Page 16 - 17 KR08		
Spa Pool, Hamersley Gorge	Circular Pool, Dales Gorge	Circular Pool, Dales Gorge	Circular Pool, Dales Gorge		
Page 18 KR26	Page 20 KR27	Page 22 - 23 KR28	Page 24 - 25 KR29	Page 21 KR33	Page 24 KR34
Fortescue Falls, Dales Gorge	'Ferns' Dales Gorge	'Roots' Dales Gorge	Fern Pool (cover image is KR30)	Fortescue Falls	Fern Pool
Page 27 - 28 KR16	Page 28 KR09	Page 30 - 31 KR17	Page 32 - 33 KR31		
'Karjini Reflections'	Kermit's Pool, Hancock Gorge	'Cascade of Colour' Hancock Gorge	'Colours Within'		
Page 34 - 35 KR04	Page 42 - 43 KR21	Page 44 - 45 KR19	Page 48 - 49 KR06	Page 29 KR24	Page 36 KR22
Regan's Pool, Hancock Gorge	'Last Light' Hancock Gorge	Mt Bruce	Handrail Pool, Weano Gorge	Kermit's Pool	Kermit's Pool
Page 50 - 51 KR10	Page 56 - 57 KR12	Page 60 - 61 KR11	Page 62 - 63 PR01		
'Last Pool' Weano Gorge	Hamersley Range	Cliff Lookout, Millstream N.P.	Mt Nameless, Tom Price		

64   Visual Index & Print Catalogue (These images are available as prints from the Ben Knapinski online gallery - *www.bjk.com.au*)